Carla   Livia   Francesco   Franz   Elisa

This atlas was developed in collaboration with
researchers from the National Institute for Nuclear Physics in Italy,
skilled and curious women and men
who study the extraordinary phenomena of the Universe every day.

Look for their faces in this book,
and on the last page read more about their experiences...

one day you might be one of them!

CONTENTS

THE UNIVERSE

How did we begin to learn about our Universe?

For more than two thousand years we have come to know our Universe, thanks to our observations of the light emitted by celestial bodies, such as stars or galaxies. Our instruments for observation have developed over time. We began by observing with the naked eye, and then invented binoculars and **telescopes**.

How fast does light travel?

Light from objects in the sky moves towards us at a great speed: a ray of light travels about **300,000 kilometres (186,000 miles) in one second.** When we look at a distant star, what we actually see is what that star was like a long time ago when those rays of light were emitted. Observing the skies is like looking back in time!

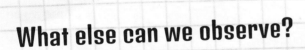

1.3 seconds

Light takes about 1.3 seconds to reach Earth from the Moon.

What else can we observe?

For millennia, light has been our only source of information about the Universe. In the last century we also learned to use **cosmic rays**, particles that propagate in Space and offer us information about the objects that emit them. In 2016 we discovered another important messenger: **gravitational waves.** So in the present day, we have the coordinate observations of a 'multi-messenger astronomy'.

Light

Cosmic rays

Gravitational waves

What theories do we use to study the Universe?

There are **four fundamental forces** in nature. The one most familiar to us is gravity, described by Albert Einstein about a century ago. The other three interactions are: strong nuclear force, weak nuclear force and electromagnetism. A theory describes these latter as the **'Standard Model'**, the existence of which scientists were able to confirm in 2012 with the discovery of the Higgs boson at CERN in Geneva.

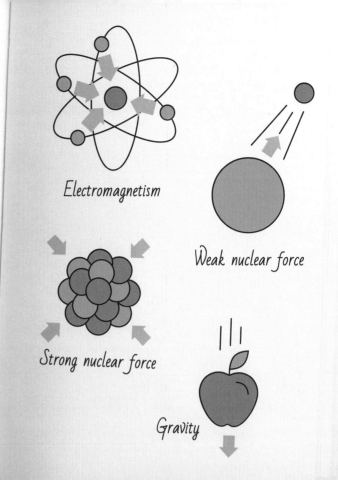

Electromagnetism

Weak nuclear force

Strong nuclear force

Gravity

The Universe expands just like an inflating balloon: as it grows, the distance between distant galaxies increases over time.

→ **Time**

Does our Universe change over time?

Yes. American astronomer **Edwin Hubble** discovered that our Universe is expanding. He observed clusters of stars, called galaxies, moving away from us: the farther away the galaxies, the greater the speed. Looking back, we can imagine that these galaxies were very close a long time ago. We can also imagine the very moment this expansion began, when matter had an infinitely large density. This initial moment, an explosion, is called the **'Big Bang'**.

THE BIG BANG

How do we know there was a Big Bang?

The Big Bang created an **incandescent Universe**
which, following expansion, cooled down.

Remnants of that original radiation were discovered in the 1960s
and are still visible today. Although we were not able to directly observe the Big Bang,
we can observe its 'echo'!

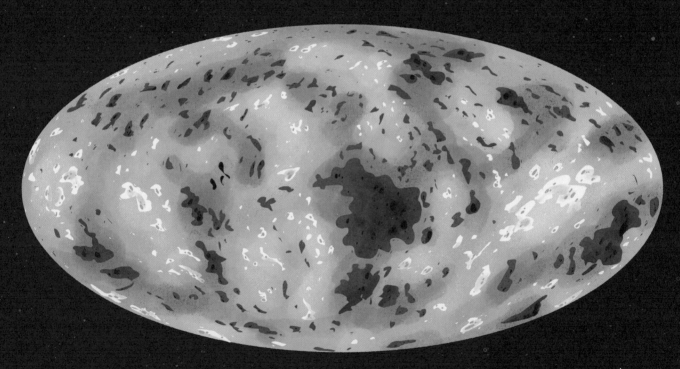

Map of the 'cosmic microwave background', the radiation remaining in the
Universe from the Big Bang, measured for the first time in 1965.

How long ago did the Big Bang take place?

By combining scientists' theories with data from astronomical observations,
we can calculate that the age of our Universe
(the time that has passed since the Big Bang) is about 14 billion years!

⑥ How were galaxies born?

600 million years after the Big Bang
The early Universe was not completely homogeneous: there were little differences in density. Matter in the lower-density regions was attracted to the higher density regions to form galaxies.

⑤ When were the first stars formed?

200 million years after the Big Bang
The first stars formed as a result of a collapse under their own gravity, about two hundred million years after the Big Bang.

④

400,000 years after the Big Bang
Much later, when the Universe was about four hundred thousand years old, nuclei and electrons joined together to form the first atoms. Then, all matter was produced in the stars through nuclear reactions.

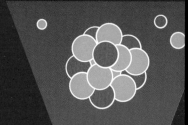

③

One second after the Big Bang
Then, about one second after the Big Bang, protons and neutrons joined together to form the nuclei of the lighter elements.

② When was matter as we know it formed?

One-millionth of a second after the Big Bang
It took different stages for the particles to become atoms. First, particles known as 'quarks' joined together to form protons and neutrons when the age of the Universe was about one-millionth of a second.

① Big Bang

14 billion years ago

THE STRUCTURE OF THE UNIVERSE

The Milky Way

Our solar system is here!

Are we at the centre of the Universe?

It seems that all the galaxies are fleeing from us, but we are not at the centre of the Universe. Someone located in another galaxy would observe the same phenomenon!

This phenomenon is similar to when a **fruit cake** rises. Let's imagine that the candied fruits are the galaxies: each one will see the others moving away in every direction, but this does not mean that it is in the centre of the cake.

So our location is nothing out of the ordinary?

Exactly! For centuries it was believed that we were at the centre of the Universe, but today we know that this is not true. Earth is only one of the planets that revolve around the Sun, and the Sun is just one of many, many stars in the galaxy, located quite far from the centre.
In the Universe, in fact, there exist **many galaxies** similar to ours.
Our position in Space, therefore, is nothing out of the ordinary!

Can we see all the matter present in the Universe?

The surprising answer to this question is: No! We know with certainty that there is a lot of matter in our Universe that is invisible, and for this reason it is called **'dark matter'**.

In fact, we know that galaxies move away from each other at a rate that increases with time. This sensational discovery—a discovery not made until 1998—shows that the expansion of our Universe is accelerating.

There must therefore be an invisible entity, what we call **dark energy**, and revealing its identity is another of the profound mysteries of our Universe yet to be uncovered!

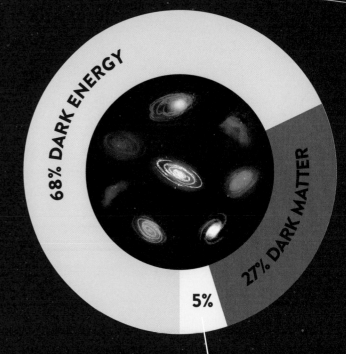

68% DARK ENERGY

27% DARK MATTER

5%

KNOWN MATTER

How do we know that something invisible exists?

Celestial bodies move because of the **force of gravity** exerted by other bodies. We know how to observe with precision the motion of visible objects and we can deduce how much gravity it takes to generate this motion. But gravity is caused by matter, so we can also calculate how much matter is needed.

We have calculated that the amount of matter needed to produce the motions of the celestial bodies is significantly higher than the matter we see. Therefore, there must be another form of matter invisible to us.

Do we know how much dark matter is present?

Invisible matter is five times denser than visible matter. Dark matter therefore makes up most of the matter in our Universe!

SPACETIME AND GRAVITATIONAL WAVES

What is spacetime?

Space and time are connected. This is because light travels at a very great speed but not infinite. So it takes time for light to travel from one point to another. Anything that moves in Space therefore also travels in time.
Together, space and time form spacetime.

Stars and planets can bend spacetime like a sphere on a blanket.

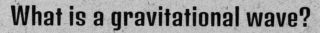

What is a gravitational wave?

It is a wave in spacetime: a wave that you cannot see, which travels at the speed of light and, as it passes, **warps everything** it encounters, alternately expanding and contracting it: just like a caramel pulled and pressed between two fingers!

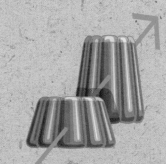

How are they measured?

Scientists have developed special instruments for measuring gravitational waves, devices known as 'interferometers'. They have the shape of an enormous 'L' into which a laser light beam is sent. The difference in the travel times of the light in the two arms is measured. If there are no gravitational waves, their difference is zero. If a gravitational wave passes through, it shortens one arm of the 'L' while it lengthens the other, and the times that the laser beams take to travel the two arms change.

Virgo interferometer in Cascina, Tuscany

Black hole

Gravitational waves

Spacetime

How are gravitational waves generated?

To produce gravitational waves it is necessary to make spacetime vibrate while changing its curvature. To produce strong gravitational waves you need a great concentration of matter, powerful acceleration and a strong measure of asymmetry. Among the most powerful sources of gravitational waves are, for instance, stellar explosions, or the systems of two stars or two black holes revolving around each other and then merging.

But do they really exist?

Of course! The first wave was measured in 2015 by two LIGO interferometers in the United States. Virgo started measuring waves in 2017. Measuring these waves, however, is very difficult, because their effects are very small! Thanks to these measurements we are learning many previously unknown things about black holes and the Universe.

Who was the first to identify them?

Albert Einstein, the famous physicist, hypothesized the existence of gravitational waves in his theory of relativity, stating however that it would be impossible to measure them because they are too weak. Thanks to new technologies, one hundred years later, we are able to detect them!

A word from...

GALAXIES

A galaxy is a group of celestial bodies, gas and dust held together by the force of gravity.

Do you see that bright area? It is a galactic bulge, a group made up of many stars. In the centre is a black hole.

Milky Way

Our Earth is located in the galaxy known as the **Milky Way**, so named since Antiquity because of its visible trail in the sky resembling a river of milk.

Are there photographs of the 'whole' Milky Way?

No, because it is impossible to photograph something from inside of it, like trying to take a picture of your home while in your bedroom!
The images we see are usually of other spiral galaxies which are more or less the same shape as the Milky Way.

How long has the Milky Way existed?

Our galaxy is almost as old as the Universe itself, so dates back to about **13.6 billion years ago.** It is not known precisely how it formed, but most likely it rose from an initial globular cluster that gradually attracted cosmic material to itself.

How big is a galaxy?

The dimensions of galaxies vary greatly: there are dwarf galaxies, and giant ones, with a thousand billion stars... The Milky Way has a diameter of about 100,000 light years. Just think, a light year corresponds to about 9,500 billion kilometres (5,900 billion miles)!

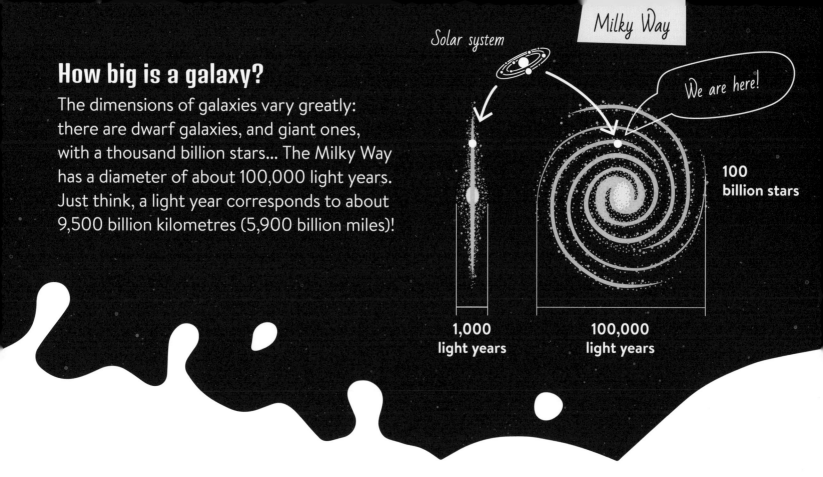

Solar system

Milky Way

We are here!

100 billion stars

1,000 light years

100,000 light years

What shape does a galaxy have?

There is a great variety: there are galaxies that are irregular, elliptical, normal spiral and barred spiral. The Milky Way is a barred spiral galaxy: this means that it has a central core crossed by a sort of bar that extends into two curved arms. We are located in one of these arms.

Irregular   *Elliptical*   *Spiral*   *Barred spiral*

Did you know that galaxies move?

Well, yes. Like all objects in the Universe, even the stars that compose the galaxies move, orbiting around its centre. The average **galactic rotation** is between 210 and 240 km/s (130-149 mi/s). Galaxies even 'collide': the Milky Way, in this way, has 'devoured' other galaxies...

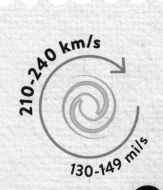

210-240 km/s

130-149 mi/s

STARS

The stars are enormous spheres of incandescent gas.
From Earth, we see them as many little luminous points in the sky.

Earth
> 149,600,000 km
> 93,000,000 mi

How far away are the stars?

The closest star to Earth is **the Sun**, 149,600,000 kilometres (93,000,000 mi) away. Try to imagine how very far away that is, but the Sun still manages to warm us! The other stars are much more distant, even tens of light years from Earth.

electromagnetic waves

98% H + He

What is a star composed of?

Largely **hydrogen and helium**, which together make up about 98%, but also, in smaller quantities, metals. However, stars change over time. The older a star is, the smaller its metallic component.

 From 20 km to 1 billion km

How big are they? And how many are there?

The smallest stars have a diameter of about 20 kilometres (12 miles), while the largest can reach one billion kilometres! As for quantity...nobody knows! We know only that there are **hundreds of billions** of them in a single galaxy.

Why do stars shine?

Stars—and therefore the Sun—emit **energy** in the form of electromagnetic waves. It is precisely this energy that makes stars bright!

Are the stars all the same?

No! Each star goes through **different stages of life**.

Stars with a mass similar to that of the Sun tend to expand and cool down from 'red giants' to 'white dwarfs'.

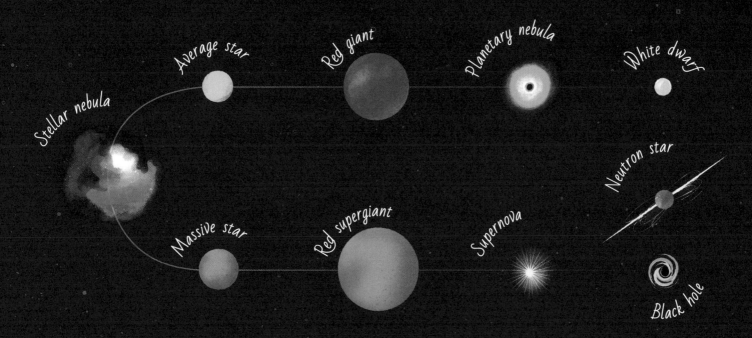

Stars larger than the Sun evolve into 'red supergiants' and collapse. Sometimes they become huge 'supernovae', which either explode leaving only the nucleus intact ('neutron star') or transform into a black hole.

What is a constellation?

It is a group of stars that, viewed from Earth, form a recognizable shape.

The most famous constellations are the 'zodiac': Aries, Taurus, Gemini, Cancer, Leo, Virgo, Libra, Scorpio, Sagittarius, Capricorn, Aquarius and Pisces. Also among the most recognizable constellations are Ursa Major and Ursa Minor.

METEOR, ASTEROID AND COMET

These three types of celestial bodies are always confused. Let's clear things up a little!

What is a meteor?

In Space different bodies of rock move. Ones similar to small boulders are called **meteoroids**.

Meteoroid

When a meteoroid crosses the atmosphere of a planet, it becomes a meteor. Meteors that ignite and leave a trail are commonly called shooting stars.

Can a meteorite fall on your head?

In theory... yes! Earth is bombarded every day by meteorites, which fortunately for the most part are very small. It is estimated that about 500 meteorites reach the surface of our planet every year. Many of these, however, are lost in the sea or desert.

Meteor

Meteorite

Meteorites, unlike meteors, are the rocky fragments that 'survive' the passage in the atmosphere.

Asteroid

What is an asteroid?

An **asteroid** is a rocky or metallic body larger than a meteoroid: it is almost a small planet, but with an irregular shape.

What is a comet?

Comets are similar to asteroids, but are predominantly composed of **ice**. Precisely for this reason, when a comet approaches the Sun it begins to 'sublimate', that is, to pass directly from the solid to the gaseous state, forming a trail. **Attention: comets are not stars!**

Comet

The luminous trail that follows the comet is formed by **gas** or **dust**: in the first, its colour is white-blue, while in the second, yellowish. The shapes can also be different: similar to a needle or a sword, long or short...

Atmosphere

Earth

Is it correct to say 'shooting star'?

In reality a 'shooting star' does not exist!
In fact, comets are not stars. That they shine like moving stars is due precisely to the sublimation of the ice, which we admire when a comet passes close enough to Earth.

THE SOLAR SYSTEM

Interstellar dust

Comets

Asteroids

What is a planetary system made of?

As its name indicates, a planetary system is made up of planets, but also satellites, asteroids and comets. Surrounding the major bodies is interstellar dust, consisting of small particles of matter and gas aggregated in more or less dense clouds.

Saturn

Sun

Neptune

Mercury

How big is the solar system?

The solar system has no precise boundaries, but its diameter is approximately **80 times** the distance that separates Earth from the Sun.

To calculate its size we therefore multiply **80 x 149,600,000 kilometres (93,000,000 miles).**

We're going to need a very powerful calculator!

Venus

A planetary system is a group of objects that revolve around a star. The centre of our planetary system, in which Earth is located, is the Sun, and therefore our system is called 'solar'.

Uranus

Jupiter

Mars

How was the solar system formed?

Our planetary system originated about **4.7 billion years ago** from a nebula of hydrogen, helium and dust. Due to gravitational force, the nebula collapsed on itself, condensing the particles in the centre and forming a disc extending over 10 billion kilometres (6.2 billion miles). The core heated up, which created the Sun.

Earth

How many planetary systems are there in the Universe?

We do not know, but there are certainly different planetary systems in each galaxy. So far, more than 2,700 planetary systems have been catalogued, for a total of around **3,700 exoplanets**.

Is it possible to leave the solar system?

Of course, even if the travel times are really, really long.

Imagine, the **Voyager 1** space probe, launched by the United States in 1977, is still on its way. It is the farthest man-made object from Earth.

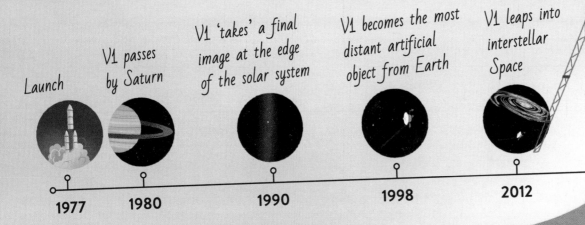

Launch

V1 passes by Saturn

V1 'takes' a final image at the edge of the solar system

V1 becomes the most distant artificial object from Earth

V1 leaps into interstellar Space

Voyager 1

1977   1980   1990   1998   2012

How many celestial bodies are there in the solar system?

In addition to the Sun and the planets, the solar system contains many celestial bodies of different types: asteroids, satellites, gas and dust.

146 SATELLITES

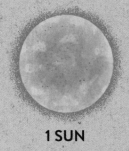

We can count the largest 'objects':
there is one Sun,
8 planets and 146 satellites.
Our natural satellite is the Moon!

8 PLANETS

1 SUN

Why is 'Space' black?

Space is completely dark because... there is no air! On Earth, the sun's rays diffuse in all directions because of the presence of the atmosphere, while in Space the 'void' causes light to travel in a straight line, without diffusing.

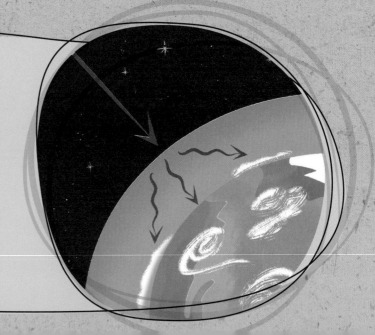

How long does a year last in the solar system?

The time we calculate on Earth, once it has passed our atmosphere, no longer exists!

Our subdivision into hours, days, months and years, in fact, is the result of a **convention** based on the movement of our planet.

This is why time is 'different' on other planets.

1 YEAR
One year is the time it takes for Earth to revolve around the Sun.

Jupiter
12 years

Mercury
88 days

Mars
687 days

Earth
365 days

Venus
225 days

Neptune
165 years

Saturn
30 years

Uranus
84 years

Is there life in the solar system (beyond us)?

Difficult to say: the search for life on other planets is ongoing. For now we are looking for the presence of water in the solar system, because **water is essential to the existence of life forms.**

We know that millions of years ago water existed on Venus and Mars, and that some natural satellites once had oceans... So it is not out of the question that, sometime in the future, we will be able to positively answer this question!

According to some hypotheses, this is how Venus looked millions of years ago. Doesn't it remind you a little of our Earth?

This, however, is currently what Venus looks like (inhospitable!). But just think, in 2020, 'phosphine' was discovered in its atmosphere, a gas that testifies to past biological activity.

THE SUN

The Sun is the closest star to Earth, and it is at the centre of the solar system. It is the presence of the Sun that illuminates and allows life on our planet!

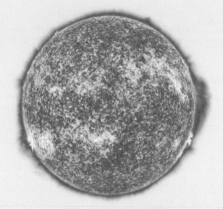

 149,600,000 km
(93,000,000 mi)

 8 minutes

What is the distance between the Sun and Earth?

The average distance between our planet and the Sun is 149,600,000 kilometres (93,000,000 miles).

This measurement is called the **'astronomical unit'** and is used to define the distances between celestial bodies.

Just think, sunlight takes about 8 minutes to reach Earth!

Forms of life on our planet would not exist without the Sun's light and heat, which activate biological processes.

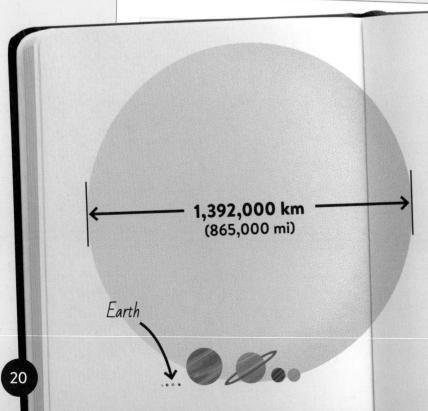

1,392,000 km
(865,000 mi)

Earth

How big is the Sun?

The Sun's diameter measures 1,392,000 kilometres (865,000 miles).

Our star is, therefore,

116 times
bigger than Earth!

If it looks enormous to you, just imagine, it is considered a small to medium star. In the Universe there are much larger stars!

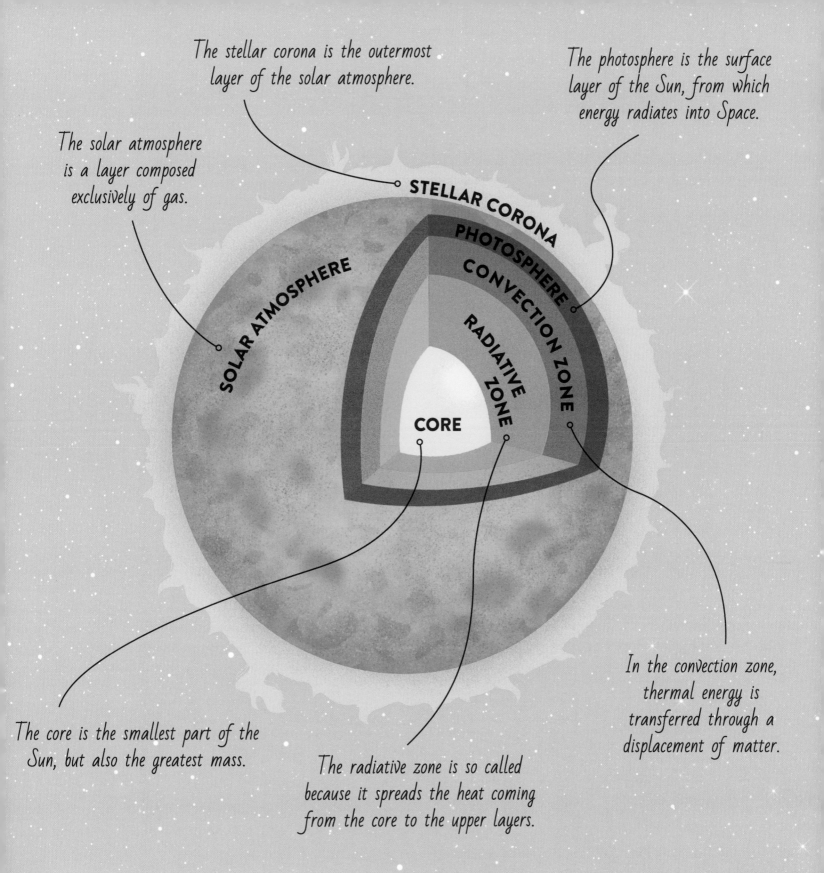

The stellar corona is the outermost layer of the solar atmosphere.

The photosphere is the surface layer of the Sun, from which energy radiates into Space.

The solar atmosphere is a layer composed exclusively of gas.

STELLAR CORONA

PHOTOSPHERE

CONVECTION ZONE

SOLAR ATMOSPHERE

RADIATIVE ZONE

CORE

The core is the smallest part of the Sun, but also the greatest mass.

The radiative zone is so called because it spreads the heat coming from the core to the upper layers.

In the convection zone, thermal energy is transferred through a displacement of matter.

How is the Sun formed?

The Sun is a rotating sphere composed of gas, mainly hydrogen and helium.
Its form is made up of different strata, like the layers of a chocolate custard doughnut.

What kind of star is the Sun?

The Sun is a **yellow dwarf** and is the colour of a very intense white.

If the Sun's surface seems peaceful and quiet to you, don't be fooled: there are powerful nuclear reactions and explosions of gases occurring, as forceful as millions of atomic bombs.

What is its temperature?

The Sun's surface reaches about **5,400 °C (9,800 °F)**: a truly incredible heat!

This is why, despite the distance between our planet and the Sun, the summer rays can still burn us!

What are sunspots?

On the surface of the Sun are colder areas, with intense magnetic activity.

These areas are a little less bright, called **'sunspots'**.

They are very big—on average about the same size as Earth! But they are only temporary.

Yellow dwarf

5,400 °C (9,800 °F)

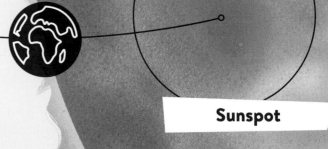

Sunspot

What is solar wind?

Solar wind is a kind of 'current' that expands from the stellar corona. This **wind of protons and electrons** reaches a temperature of a million degrees. It is so powerful that it can cause significant **magnetic perturbations**, capable of altering the functioning of artificial satellites.

Luckily, our planet is able to 'defend' itself from these solar particles thanks to the **magnetic field** that surrounds it.

How does a solar eclipse occur?

We know that Earth and the Moon move around the Sun: but what happens when these three celestial bodies find themselves perfectly aligned?

When the Moon is precisely between Earth and the Sun, it can cover all or part of the solar disc, creating the phenomenon of an eclipse.

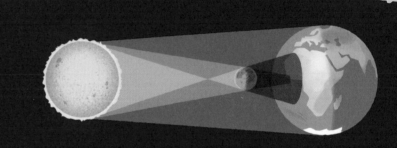

From Earth, we see a dark sphere (the Moon) surrounded by a thin disc of light (the Sun).

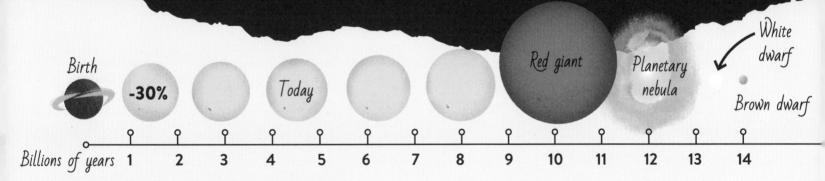

Birth

-30%

Today

Red giant

Planetary nebula

White dwarf

Brown dwarf

Billions of years 1 2 3 4 5 6 7 8 9 10 11 12 13 14

And if the Sun extinguishes?

Rather than 'if', it is a question of 'when'! Our star, in fact, is going through an evolutionary cycle that will end **in about 5 billion years**. Over time, the Sun will increase in size to become a red giant, then contract and cool into a white dwarf, smaller than the size of Earth.

THE PLANETS

In our solar system, the planets revolve around the Sun, each at a precise distance. It is the sun's force of gravity that keeps all the celestial bodies in orbit and maintains order!

How many planets are there?

The planets of our solar system are listed below. In the whole Universe, however, there are many more, even if we do not know them yet!

15.000 km (9,300 mi)

MERCURY
Mercury is the smallest planet!

VENUS

EARTH

MARS

440,000 km (273,000 mi)

JUPITER
Jupiter is the largest planet!

8 months

How big is a planet?

The smallest planet is Mercury, with a circumference of approximately 15,000 kilometres (9,320 miles).
The circumference of the largest planet, Jupiter, is almost 440,000 kilometres (273,000 miles).
Just think, the Sun has a circumference of...
4,379,000 kilometres (2,721,000 miles)!
It would take a jet almost eight months to travel completely around the Sun.

What is a planet?

A planet is a large spherical celestial body, composed of rock and gas, that revolves around a star.

Mars

RED
Iron oxide

Earth

BLUE
Water

Venus

YELLOW
Clouds of sulfuric acid

What colours are the planets?

Their colours depend on their composition. For example, Mars is called

the red planet

because it contains much iron oxide. Earth, on the other hand, is mostly blue, because it is mostly covered in water.

SATURN

URANUS

NEPTUNE

How fast do the planets revolve around the Sun?

The time it takes a planet to complete one full revolution around the Sun is called a 'year'.

For us on Earth, this period is 365 days.

Our planet revolves around the Sun at a speed of almost **30 kilometres (19 miles) per second.**

Which planet is farthest from the Sun?

Neptune is the planet farthest from the Sun, so it is a very cold planet. The temperature of its high-altitude clouds is around **-220 °C (428 °F)**!

How much do we weigh on Jupiter?

Our weight depends on the force of attraction the planet exerts on our body.

Therefore a 30 kg (66 lbs) child on Jupiter would weigh about 70 kg (154 lbs)!

30 kg (66 lbs)

70 kg (154 lbs)

And on the other planets?

Mercury	Venus	Earth	Mars	Jupiter	Saturn	Uranus	Neptune
11 kg	**27 kg**	**30 kg**	**11 kg**	**70 kg**	**33 kg**	**27 kg**	**34 kg**
(24 lbs)	(60 lbs)	(66 lbs)	(24 lbs)	(154 lbs)	(72 lbs)	(60 lbs)	(75 lbs)

WHY DOES SATURN HAVE RINGS?

Saturn's rings are composed of a great quantity of **ice** fragments that surround the planet, attracted by its gravity.

These fragments are perhaps what remain of an ancient moon of Saturn, which would have 'crumbled'.

Which is the hottest planet in the solar system?

Venus is the hottest planet in the solar system, reaching 462 degrees (864 °F)! Even though Mercury is closest to the Sun, it cannot hold solar radiation because of its lack of atmosphere. Rather, anywhere on Venus we experience the same heat.

462 °C (864 °F)

Which is the most inhospitable planet?

Not the easiest question to answer, it is probably Venus, due to its high temperature and its atmosphere composed mainly of **carbon dioxide.**

However, the other planets are also dangerous. On Mars the ground is arid and there are violent **sandstorms.** On Jupiter, columns of **gas** erupt and electromagnetic bombardment is so intense we would immediately die from the **radiation...**

Do the planets rotate all in the same direction?

No. Venus and Uranus rotate in a reverse direction to that of Earth: clockwise.

On these planets, therefore, **the Sun rises in the west and sets in the east!**

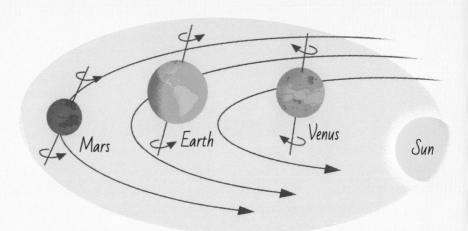

Mars   Earth   Venus   Sun

What happened to Pluto?

It is smaller than our Moon!

Pluto did not disappear into thin air! Simply, Pluto for a long time now has not been classified as a planet. In fact, it has neither the characteristics of a terrestrial planet nor of a gas planet; it is so small it is called a 'dwarf planet'.

THE MOON

The Moon is the only natural satellite of our planet. We terrestrials can admire the Moon at night in many different forms... Let's find out why!

How big is the Moon?

The Moon has an average diameter of **3,472 kilometres (2,157 miles)**. That makes it almost four times smaller than Earth.

EARTH
12,742 km
(7,917 mi)

MOON
3,472 km
(2,157 mi)

Among the natural satellites, however, the Moon is quite large: most satellites are less than 500 kilometres (311 miles) in diameter. Imagine, some are only 10 kilometres (6 miles)... just like asteroids.

How far is it from Earth?

The Moon orbits at a distance of **385,000 kilometres (239,000 miles)** from Earth.

It is the closest celestial body to our planet, and can complete a revolution in about 29 days.

Its orbit is not circular, but slightly elliptical.

385,000 km
239,000 mi

29 days

Ellipse

What is it made of?

The lunar crust is solid and composed of different **chemical elements: uranium, magnesium, potassium, silicon, thorium, iron, aluminium...**

What is a natural satellite?

It is a natural celestial body that orbits an object of larger mass, but different from a star, such as a planet or an asteroid.

There are about 150 natural satellites in the solar system.

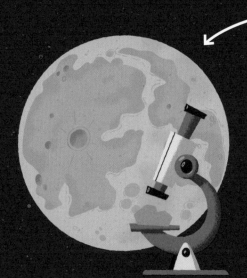

Lunar soil is grey and dusty, sprinkled with dust and clay.

The Moon has a very irregular surface, because it has been bombarded by so many asteroids: it therefore has craters interspersed with 'seas', vast flat areas.

Why does the Moon change shape?

As the Moon turns in orbit around Earth, its position to the Sun changes, making different sections of the Moon visible at different times.
Each of these times is called a **'lunar phase'**.

There are four basic phases...
... with as many intermediate phases.

1. **New moon**
2. Waxing crescent
3. **First quarter**
4. Waxing gibbous
5. **Full moon**
6. Waning gibbous
7. **Last quarter**
8. Waning crescent

The Moon's orbit illuminated by the Sun

1 2 3 4 5 6 7 8

Phases of the Moon in the northern hemisphere

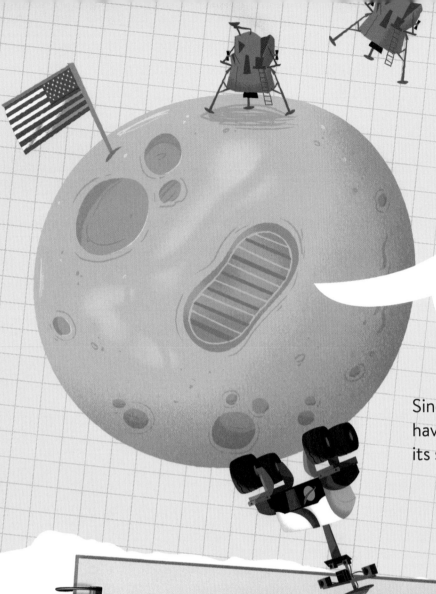

Can you walk on the Moon?

Certainly! The first mission that landed humankind on the Moon happened on **20 July 1969**.

Astronaut Neil Armstrong was the first person to step onto our satellite and take a 'walk'.

Since then, vehicles, known as 'rovers', have been sent to the Moon to study its surface, and

12 astronauts

have travelled there, all Americans.

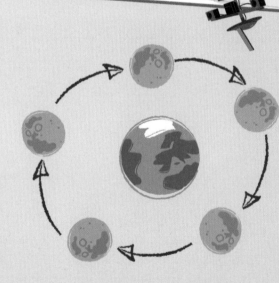

Why does the Moon have a 'dark side'?

We always see the same side of the Moon: the other side is hidden from us.

This phenomenon is due to the **synchronous rotation and revolution** with Earth.

That is, the Moon completes a rotation at the same time it completes a revolution around Earth. Therefore, the same side is always facing our planet.

Probes, however, successfully landed on the hidden side and sent back images.

What is a lunar eclipse?

Just like a solar eclipse, the lunar eclipse depends on the alignment of **Earth, Sun and Moon**. It is an optical phenomenon that occurs when Earth is positioned precisely between the Sun and the Moon, so that the Moon is in Earth's shadow.

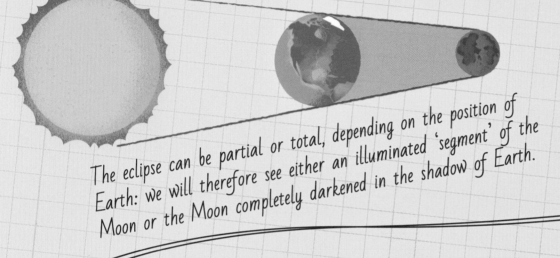

The eclipse can be partial or total, depending on the position of Earth: we will therefore see either an illuminated 'segment' of the Moon or the Moon completely darkened in the shadow of Earth.

What is the Moon's influence on Earth?

The phases of the Moon affect the tides, the changes in sea level. In reality it is not only the Moon that has an effect on the water, but the force of attraction that the Moon and the Sun exert together on Earth.

Generally, the tide is high in the part of Earth facing the Moon or on the opposite side of it, while in the rest of the planet the tide is low and going out.

Are there other moons in the Universe?

Naturally! Among the approximately **150 natural satellites** of the solar system, several are moons. Mercury and Venus are the only planets that do not have satellites.

Jupiter and Saturn have the most:

Jupiter has almost 70, and Saturn 60.

EXTREME UNIVERSE

Some of the most energetic and violent phenomena in all the Universe are the explosive deaths of the stars, jets of particles by the galaxies, gamma-ray bursts and black holes.

How do we study them?

To study these very particular celestial events, scientists have learned to use special telescopes, capable of detecting signals invisible to the eye. In fact, there exists not only visible light but also other waves and rays. For example, particles called cosmic rays come from Space. The most numerous are neutrinos and protons.

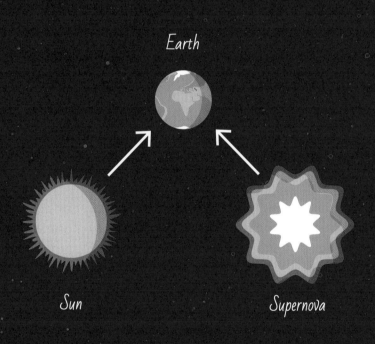

Earth

Sun

Supernova

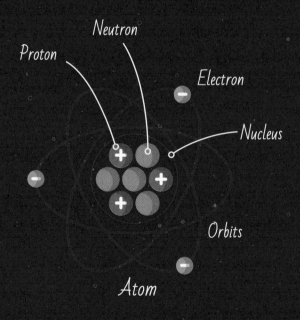

Neutron

Proton

Electron

Nucleus

Orbits

Atom

What is a neutrino?

A neutrino is a **very light** particle that travels **very fast**, almost at the speed of light. Its particular characteristic is that it is quite good at not being caught, so it is very difficult to see it with a telescope! We need enormous detectors to be able to see some of them.

What is a proton?

A proton is a very important particle for the Universe: everything we see is made of protons and other particles called neutrons and electrons. These three particles together form **atoms** and thus constitute matter: your book, your body, and even the stars.

BLACK HOLES

What is a black hole?

A black hole is an area of Space with very high density, in which a large mass is concentrated in a small space. This causes the gravitational attraction to be very powerful in its vicinity, so powerful that even light is 'sucked in'.

How much does a black hole weigh?

There are black holes for all tastes! From giant black holes, known as supermassive, which weigh as much as a billion suns, to 'small' black holes, known as stellar, which weigh ten times our Sun. Scientists are searching for even smaller black holes, called mini black holes.

How is a black hole created?

The black holes we understand the best, stellar black holes, are the remnants of very large stars, or 'massive stars', at the end of their life. What about other types of black holes? In the case of enormous black holes, scientists are still trying to understand their origin...

Where do black holes 'live'?

The black holes we observe live in galaxies. Stellar black holes live among the stars, while supermassive black holes are found, instead, at the centre of a galaxy. It seems every galaxy has a black hole, even ours!

SUPERNOVAS

If the mass of a star is more than eight times the mass of the Sun, its end will not be tranquil, because it will die with a very powerful explosion.

The phenomena of nuclear fusion continue until the star's fuel runs out and the gas contracts until it collapses. At this point the star explodes, transforming into a super-bright supernova.

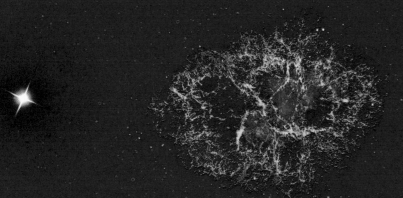

> The energy produced during a supernova explosion is truly enormous: the star becomes so bright it shines more than an entire galaxy!

> A supernova is therefore a star of great mass that explodes. Within it, the lighter elements burn producing increasingly heavier elements. Eventually what is left is an iron core that can no longer resist the force of gravity and begins to collapse.

What remains after the explosion?

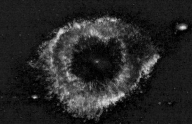

Neutron star

If the star that explodes has a mass of less than 20 solar masses, a new neutron star is formed in the centre of the explosion, with an incredibly dense mass.

Black hole

When an even more massive star dies, however, a black hole is formed.

Nebula

We can also often observe the remains of a supernova in the form of clouds of gas (nebulae).

How does a neutron star form?

When a star dies, due to the very strong gravitational attraction the elements inside the nucleus merge with each other to form matter made up of only neutrons. A **neutron** is a particle similar to a proton, but without an electric charge.

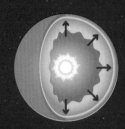
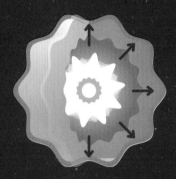

How big is a neutron star?

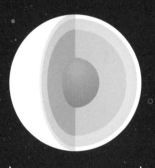

A neutron star has a mass of about one and a half times the mass of the Sun. However, the size of these stars is only a few tens of kilometres. Their density is so great that a teaspoon of 'neutron star' weighs as much as a few billion tons: around 1,000 times the pyramid of Giza!

10-20 km
(6-12 mi)

Do we know of different types?

Yes. **Pulsars**, for example, rotate a thousand times per second and are generally found in a system with another star. They are parts of older systems, and their 'companion' stars cause them to rotate at an accelerated speed. Individual 'young' neutron stars, on the other hand, initially rotate only hundreds of times per second.

SPACE EXPLORATION

Humans have always been fascinated with Space, designing instruments to explore the Universe and have a closer look!

How did space exploration begin?

It began from observation! In fact, humans have studied the sky since ancient times.

The great leap forward was the invention of the telescope, perfected by **Galileo**. It was not until the 1900s, however, that experiments to reach Space began.

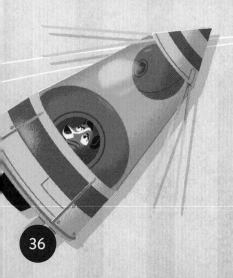

What was the first journey in Space?

The first objects to pass beyond Earth's atmosphere were the German **V2** missiles.

The first vehicle to make a full orbit around Earth was **Sputnik 1**, launched in **1957** by the Soviet Union.

Who was the first living being to enter Space?

It wasn't a human, but... a dog! On 3 November **1957**, the Soviet Union launched the **Sputnik 2** capsule into orbit, with a dog on board, who unfortunately died just a few hours after launch.

Laika

Who was the first human to enter orbit?

Soviet cosmonaut **Jurij Gagarin** is the first human to fly into outer space, aboard **Vostok 1**, launched on 12 April **1961**. Gagarin was able to complete an entire orbit around Earth and was the first human in the world to see Earth from Space.

Valentina Tereskova

And the first woman in Space?

Soviet cosmonaut **Valentina Tereskova** took off on 16 June **1963** aboard the **Vostok 6**. Her mission lasted almost three days, during which she orbited Earth.

How has space travel changed?

After Gagarin's mission, the United States launched a 'Space Race' against the Soviet Union. In **1969** the United States was the first to reach the Moon with the Apollo program. The first human to set foot on the surface of the Moon was **Neil Armstrong**, who pronounced the famous phrase: 'That's one small step for a man, one giant leap for mankind.'

'That's one small step for a man, one giant leap for mankind.'

SPACE VEHICLES

There are different types of vehicles able to travel through Space, including those without a crew and those made for transporting people.

What is a space probe?

Crewless vehicles are mostly **exploration vehicles**.
A space probe is an example, equipped with observation instruments and an antenna to communicate with Earth.

A probe is transported into orbit by means of a launch vehicle, or **'carrier rocket'**, which releases the probe at a calculated trajectory.

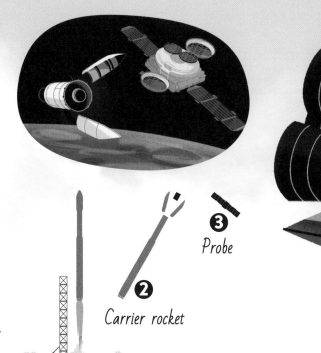

❸ Probe

❷ Carrier rocket

❶

What is the difference between a probe and a space capsule?

Probes are used to study Space and each has a specific task.
For example, Mariner 4 was the first probe to reach Mars.
The space capsule, on the other hand, is designed to carry a crew.

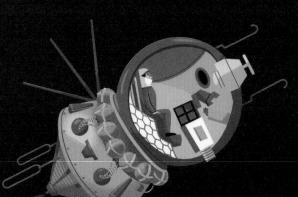

Gagarin's Vostok 1 was a space capsule. Imagine, the module that housed the cosmonaut measured just over two metres in diameter!

What are the most famous space vehicles?

From the 1960s to the present day, some of the most widely used vehicles for the transport of astronauts are those of the **Soyuz** programme, initially developed by the Soviet Union.

Until 2011, however, the famous **Space Shuttle** was also used, very similar to an airplane!

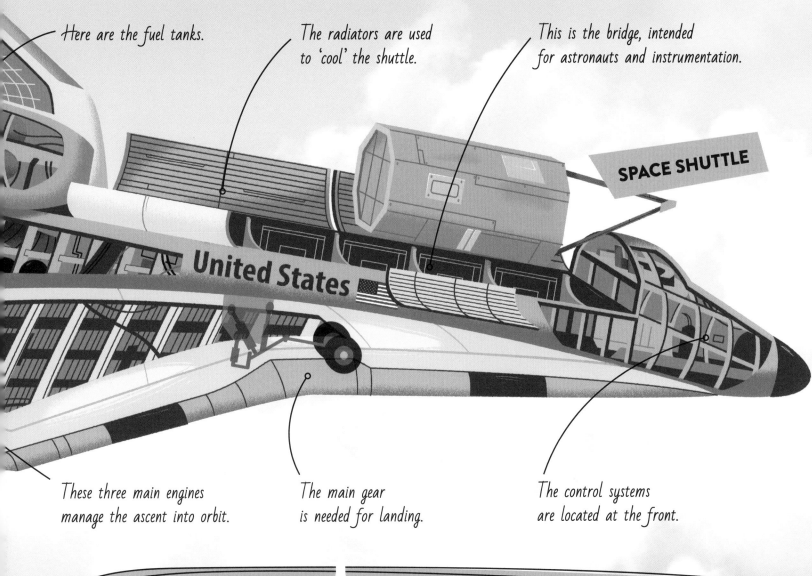

Here are the fuel tanks.

The radiators are used to 'cool' the shuttle.

This is the bridge, intended for astronauts and instrumentation.

SPACE SHUTTLE

United States

These three main engines manage the ascent into orbit.

The main gear is needed for landing.

The control systems are located at the front.

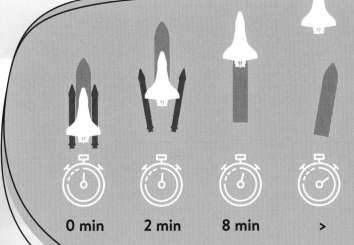

0 min   2 min   8 min   >

How was a Space Shuttle made?

A **Shuttle** consisted of an Orbiter (with the astronauts and cargo), two rockets that are disengaged two minutes after launch, and a large external tank. What you see here is the **Orbiter**!

ARTIFICIAL SATELLITES

We have already seen that in the Universe there are different natural satellites, or celestial objects, that revolve around the planets. But do you know that humans are also able to build them?

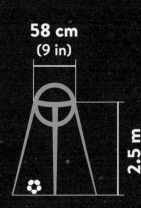

58 cm (9 in)

2.5 m (8.2 ft)

83 kg (183 lbs)

How did the first artificial satellite come to be?

1957

The first satellite sent into orbit by humankind was Sputnik 1, launched in 1957. Thanks to the data collected by the satellite, it was possible to obtain important information about the atmosphere. Thousands of artificial satellites have been launched since then!

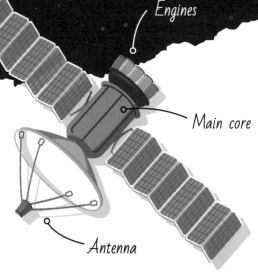

Solar panels

Engines

Main core

Antenna

How is an artificial satellite made?

Sputnik 1 was a metal sphere just 60 centimetres (24 inches) in diameter. Today satellites are more complex, but they always have a main core and a series of antennas and cameras for transmitting data. They also have solar panels, used for obtaining energy.

Can astronauts be on artificial satellites?

Yes, but in this case, rather than satellites, these are orbital space stations, habitable and equipped with on-board guidance systems.

How does a satellite work?

A satellite is sent into orbit by means of a 'carrier'. Each satellite uses antennas and cameras to collect and exchange data with Earth, where powerful computers process the information instant by instant.

What are satellites for?

There are different types of satellites and with different functions! Telecommunications, geolocation, weather forecasting...

When we use a GPS to orient ourselves, we rely on the work of satellites that can determine **the position** of a vehicle, plane or ship.

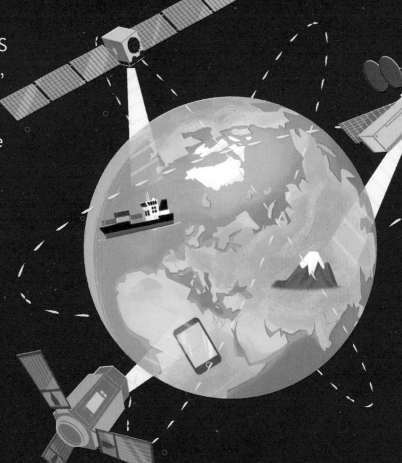

Other satellites observe Earth's surface: study its nature, degrees of pollution, the state of the ice... This is what is known as '**remote sensing**'.

Telecommunications satellites can connect two or more points on Earth, even those very distant from each other. In fact, we use satellites when we call abroad!

ASTRONAUTS

How do you become an astronaut?

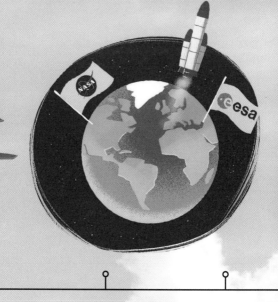

First, you must earn a **degree** in a science (such as physics or engineering) and know English.

Then, you must have flight experience as a **pilot** and a **diving** license. In addition, you must be between 25 and 40 years of age, between 153 and 190 cm (5'0"-6'3") tall and have excellent vision.

If you meet these requirements, you may present yourself for selection at a **space agency**, such as the ESA or NASA.

How is a spacesuit made?

The spacesuit is 10 centimetres thick and has 11 layers of synthetic and metallic materials.

The spacesuit protects the astronauts from the conditions of Space, which would otherwise be lethal.

A spacesuit must be flexible but also resistant to changes in pressure and temperature; it must protect the astronauts and provide them with oxygen.

The main actors in space exploration are: astronauts!
These are people who have studied long and hard and have undergone specialized training.

What does 'astronaut' mean? It comes from the Greek language and literally means 'sailor of the stars'. Poetic, don't you think?

If you are selected, you will undergo a series of **examinations**: psychological tests, medical **assessments** and **interviews**. It is essential that you are healthy and strong.

Once you are selected for a space mission, you undergo a long period of **preparation**. You will study space technologies and learn to perform activities in zero gravity.

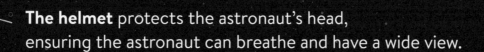

The helmet protects the astronaut's head, ensuring the astronaut can breathe and have a wide view.

The gloves are reinforced to prevent them from being punctured or cut.

On the chest the suit has **controls** to manage temperature, pressure, communication and other functions.

Astronauts are sealed inside their suits: that is why they also wear **diapers**!

Also known as ISS, the station is an enormous space laboratory that orbits our planet.

How did the ISS begin?

The project began in **1984**, proposed by the United States, to create a space programme that included different countries around the world.
Europe, Japan and Canada joined that year, and Russia followed in 1993.

Under construction since 1998, it is the largest orbiting artificial object ever built by humans.

Service module

How is it designed?

The ISS is made up of several **modules.**
Different modules contain the scientific laboratories and the instrumentation and others connect the space capsules and house the living quarters.

Huge **solar panels** convert the light of the sun into electric energy.

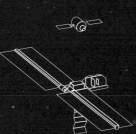

Solar panels

SPACE STATION

How big is the ISS?

As big as a football field.
It is so big that it can be seen
from Earth with the naked eye!

Dimensions:

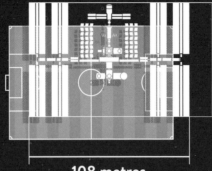

88 metres
(289 feet)

108 metres
(354 feet)

Weight:

450
tons

How far away is it from Earth? How fast does it travel?

Speed: 28,000 km/h (17,400 mi/h)

Earth

Distance:
400 km

250 mi

ISS

 Full revolution:
1.5 hours

Segmented base frame

Pressurized modules

WHAT DOES THE ISS DO?

The ISS was designed to conduct
different studies. Technologies are developed
and tested here for space exploration and for
astronauts destined for long missions.

Experiments are conducted in a
low-gravity environment and astronomic
and meteorological observations are made.

RESEARCH

Research conducted over the years on the ISS has focused on technological innovation and the study of human physiology.

For example, studies have included the **effects of weightlessness** on the nervous system and changes in cells, to learn how the human body reacts in Space over time.

Another experiment concerns the psychological effects on astronauts from staying in Space for long periods of time. For example, it was discovered that with the absence of gravity humans **lose track of time**!

Another activity that the ISS astronauts dedicate themselves to is the **cultivation of vegetation.** In 2015 red lettuce was successfully grown on board the ISS for the first time.

Do astronauts ever leave the ISS?

Sure! They have different 'extravehicular activities' (EVA), often referred to as 'spacewalks'.

How do you prepare for a spacewalk?

First, you need to check that the **spacesuits** are ready, equipped with batteries and fully-functioning life-support systems.

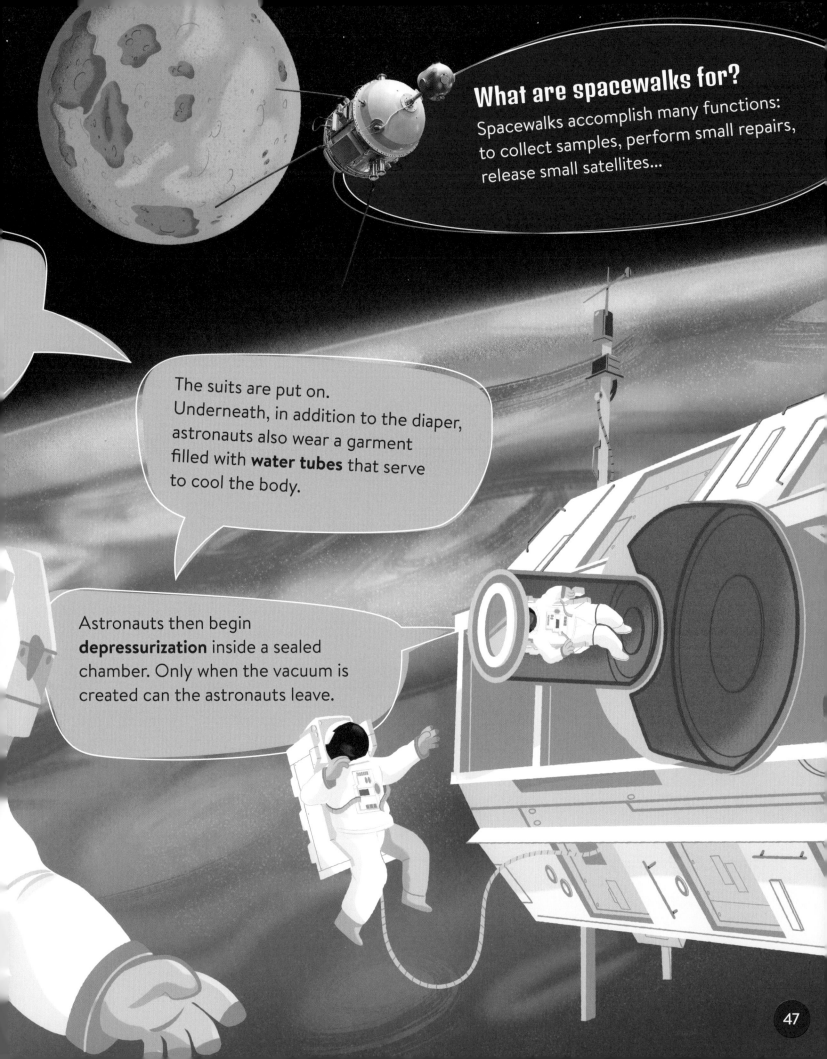

What are spacewalks for?

Spacewalks accomplish many functions: to collect samples, perform small repairs, release small satellites...

The suits are put on. Underneath, in addition to the diaper, astronauts also wear a garment filled with **water tubes** that serve to cool the body.

Astronauts then begin **depressurization** inside a sealed chamber. Only when the vacuum is created can the astronauts leave.

A TYPICAL DAY

An astronaut's day lasts 24 hours as on Earth, but within this timespan on the ISS an astronaut will see approximately 15 sunrises and as many sunsets!

6:00 AM
Wake up and breakfast.

7:30-8:00 AM
Conference with Earth, the day's work is planned.

8:15 AM
Work begins!

1:00 PM
Lunch break.

What are we eating?

It is not possible to keep fresh produce and freshly-picked vegetables... there is not only no fridge on the ISS but also no gravity!

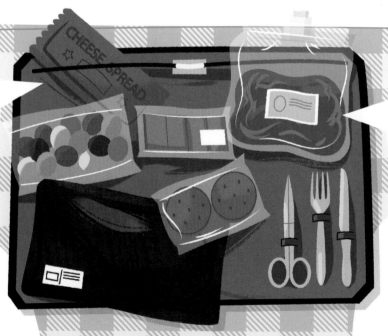

Each portion can be heated in special **ovens**.

On the ISS, food is stored in special **single-use packages** capable of staying vacuum-sealed.

If the food is **dehydrated** or **freeze-dried**, water may need to be added... but carefully!

You have to be very careful with liquids and powders: drinking therefore is through **straws**, and salt and pepper come in a dense liquid form.

2:00 PM
Work resumes.

6:00 PM
Review of the day's work and physical activity.

7:30 PM
Dinner and repose.

9:30 PM
Everyone to bed!

© NASA

How do astronauts wash?

In the absence of gravity, running water cannot be used, so astronauts wash with a special **detergent solution** that does not foam and rub off the solution with a towel.

And how do you go to the bathroom in Space? There is a special **tube** for pee that sucks in the liquid and transforms it... into drinking water!

Dirty clothes and **laundry** are enclosed in a container and thrown into Space, where they incinerate.

Where does waste go?

Just like clothing, all ISS waste is collected aboard **cargo shuttles** and dumped into Space. These containers, returning to the atmosphere, become incinerated and the contents, therefore, destroyed.

Is cleaning necessary?

Of course, it is mandatory! Dirt can damage the instrumentation. However, liquid cleaners cannot be used, nor a broom and dustpan! Cleaning is done with a **vacuum cleaner** and special pieces of fabric.

What if an astronaut feels unwell?

This would pose a problem, because the closest hospital is on Earth! That is why all astronauts learn **first aid**. Further, devices are being developed to perform ultrasound scans or to treat small ailments even in orbit.

How do astronauts sleep?

Astronauts slip into a **sleeping bag** and fasten it tightly to a wall, so they don't float away and hit something while they rest! Further, since darkness does not occur, generally **masks** are used to block out the light or the portholes are darkened.

How do astronauts relax?

In their pastime, astronauts are free to indulge in their favourite activities. Each astronaut has a **private cabin** where he or she can retire to watch a movie, use a computer, listen to music or read a book.

Is it possible to do physical activity?

Not only is it possible, it is also mandatory. In fact, the absence of gravity causes the **muscles** to lose their tone and the **heart** to weaken. However, doing gymnastics while 'floating' is not easy! So various types of equipment are used, such as bars and cables fixed to the walls.

FUTURE PROSPECTS

Scientific research is a field that evolves from day to day.
So, what will happen in the future?

Some day, will any person be able to travel in Space?

Of course: someone already has! Back in 2001 wealthy American
Dennis Tito spent seven days on the ISS for pure pleasure.
The cost of this holiday? Twenty million dollars!

Several aviation and space companies are already investing in space tourism.

Will there be 'spaceports' next to the airports?

In the future, probably yes! To bring space tourists into orbit, rockets and equipped spacecraft are needed. It is therefore likely that **launch centres** will be constructed dedicated exclusively to 'holidayers'.

Will there ever be a hotel on the Moon?

We cannot say, but there will certainly be **'hotels'** in orbit: stations just like the ISS, dedicated to overnight stays in Space. Bigelow Aerospace, for example, is building an orbiting station for tourists.

Will we ever go on holiday to other planets?

This is a bit more complicated. Certainly, it will most likely happen someday, but for now it is just theory. The entrepreneur **Elon Musk**, however, has promised to bring the first human crews to Mars within ten years, and from there tourism will not be far away!

How should a space tourist prepare?

Surely, at least in the early days, a space tourist will have to undergo a short **training** to simulate the conditions of weightlessness, spacewalks and centrifuge, and learn the essentials of flight instrumentation.

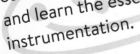

A RETURN TO THE MOON

When will we return to the Moon?

More than fifty years have passed since the first walk on the Moon by **Neil Armstrong**, and our satellite is now back at the centre of many new projects. NASA is planning to return to the Moon perhaps as early as 2024 with the Artemis program.

Artemis program

Command module

Earth

A **lunar orbital platform**, the Gateway, is already being planned and will be used as a permanent base station between Earth and Space: a bit like the ISS, but with a sort of 'lift' that goes back and forth to the Moon for closer study.

Will we ever live on our satellite?

Scientists are working on it, but the problem to be solved is the absence of an atmosphere, which makes the lunar surface openly exposed to solar radiation.

Why is the Moon so important?

The Moon is very important for space research!

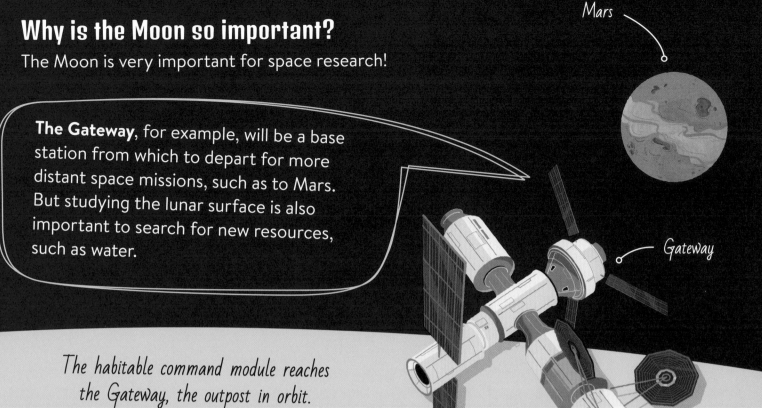

The Gateway, for example, will be a base station from which to depart for more distant space missions, such as to Mars. But studying the lunar surface is also important to search for new resources, such as water.

Mars

Gateway

The habitable command module reaches the Gateway, the outpost in orbit.

What will we do on the Moon?

As we have seen, there will be many projects: studying the lunar surface, in particular in search of **resources**; **training** astronauts destined for more-demanding missions; and **learning** how to establish settlements, for crews to remain on a permanent basis. In short, there is much to do on many fronts!

Lunar module

EXPLORATION OF MARS

Have we ever tried to go to Mars?

Of course! The first successful mission dates back to **1964** and photographs were taken of the planet from about 10,000 kilometres (6,200 miles) away. **Mars 3** was the first probe to actually land on the planet, in **1971**.

Why is it important?

Mars is crucial for research because it shows very similar characteristics to Earth. In fact, it seems that in the past there was **water** on the surface of Mars!

How long does it take to reach Mars?

The journey itself is already very long: it takes between 6 and 9 months just to reach it. Transporting a crew that far is very complex, especially refuelling vehicles for 2 to 3 years. Different rovers will be launched **between 2020 and 2022**, but it will take a little longer to send a crew.

6-9 months

How should the astronauts prepare?

The journey will be long, and it is difficult to spend so much time away from everything and everyone and closed within **confined spaces**. So, simulations are already underway, in which the astronauts, sealed in special structures, must try to... tolerate each other!

Will there ever be settlements on Mars?

Scientists are working on it... The problem to be solved once we reach the planet, however, is how to make it **habitable**. Solutions are being studied to introduce 'good' bacteria, necessary for life, or to create habitable 'capsules'.

LIVING OFF-WORLD

Will we ever live on other celestial bodies?

Difficult to say. The biggest problem is the distance. The travel time between one star and another, with our current technology, could take thousands of years.

Which celestial bodies would be 'suitable'?

The asteroids! There are several small asteroids that pass close to Earth and would therefore be easier to 'lock onto'.

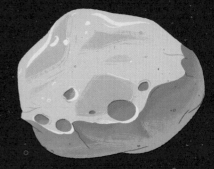

Why should we travel to other celestial bodies?

Because we could extract **valuable resources** from them. For example, private companies could mine gold, platinum and rare metals from the Moon.

Others, however, argue that it is necessary to establish settlements in Space for the **survival** of our species. If, for example, one day Earth becomes uninhabitable, we would have an escape route.

THE SEARCH FOR LIFE

Is there life in Space?

We do not have a definite answer yet! Some claim to have sighted **UFOs** or even to have encountered aliens, but nothing has been officially confirmed by the scientific community.

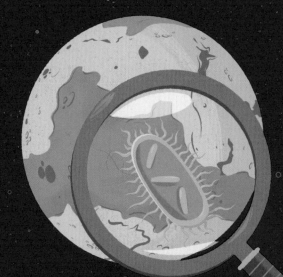

Will we ever meet an 'extraterrestrial'?

We can't be too far off! It would be enough to find a single microscopic **bacterium** for a planet to demonstrate that chemical and environmental conditions exist favourable to the development of living beings.

Star B

Will we ever find another 'Earth'?

We cannot answer for certain. However, some studies are already offering positive hypotheses. An example is a planet known as **Star B**, which appears to have environmental conditions suitable for life.

SPACE LAB

Adults can participate, too, so for all activities be sure to ask for help!

Are you ready for some hands-on fun with all the interesting facts you have learned so far?

Create your solar system!

You will need:

 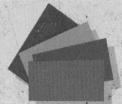     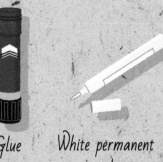

Black poster board | Poster boards of different colours | Compass | Pencil | Scissors | Glue | White permanent marker

1 Take the different-coloured poster boards and draw a circle on each with your compass, applying the following diameters:

- Mercury: 1 cm (0.5")
- Venus: 4 cm (1.5")
- Earth: 4 cm (1.5")
- Mars: 2 cm (1")
- Jupiter: 48 cm (19")
- Saturn: 38 cm (15")
- Uranus: 20 cm (8")
- Neptune: 20 cm (8")

2 Cut out each circle and write the name of the planet on it according to the size as indicated from the list. These are your planets!

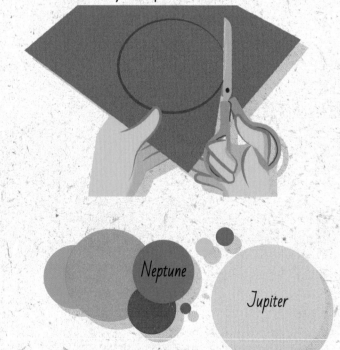

Neptune

Jupiter

3 From the yellow poster board, cut out a large crescent and glue it on the left side of the black poster board. This will be the Sun!

4 Paste the planets on the black poster board: place them in the right order as you learned from the book!

5 Trace lines with the white marker to represent the orbits. Then fill the poster board by drawing in stars, asteroids, comets, whatever you like!

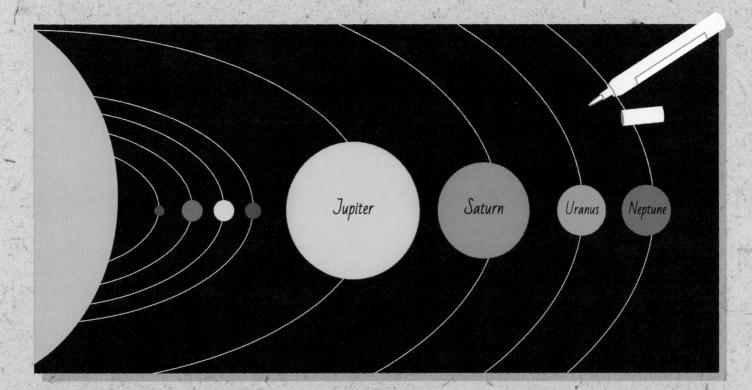

Jupiter Saturn Uranus Neptune

Draw a galaxy!

You will need:

Black
poster board

Silver glitter

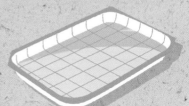

A plastic tray

Glue

White permanent
marker

1 Take the sheets of black poster board and with the glue 'draw' different shapes of galaxies: elliptical, spiral, irregular... For help with the shapes, use the images below!

2 Sprinkle the sheets with glitter, then shake the excess into the tray. Like magic, your glittering galaxies will appear!

Irregular

Elliptical

Spiral

Barred spiral

3 With your permanent marker, under each galaxy write the name of the type of galaxy it is.

Irregular galaxy

Elliptical galaxy

Spiral galaxy

Barred spiral galaxy

62

Simulate a solar eclipse

You will need:

Table lamp

Ball of modelling clay

Sheet of paper

Pencil

1 Remove the lamp shade to expose the bulb and place the lamp on a table. This will be our Sun!

2 Make a small hole in the centre of the paper with the pencil.

3 Insert the pencil into the ball of modelling clay. This will be our Moon!

4 Hold the paper in front of you and position yourself perfectly in line with the 'Sun' and 'Moon'. If you look through the hole in the paper, you will see an eclipse!

Istituto Nazionale di Fisica Nucleare

INFN, the National Institute of Nuclear Physics is the research institution in Italy that studies nature at its most elementary level. By studying the smallest components of matter, particles, and their interactions, we can find answers about the origin, characteristics and destiny of our Universe.

The INFN is present throughout Italy and works in close contact with the most important research laboratories in the world, in particular with CERN in Geneva.

INFN research requires the continual development of cutting-edge technologies, also in collaboration with industry, often with important implications for society.

INFN scientists therefore have the duty, and the pleasure, to share their work and the results of their work with society, about their research and its consequences to everyone on our planet, including you.

This book was created through collaboration with:

CARLA ARAMO

As a child Carla Aramo wanted to be a doctor, but then a desire to understand the world around us and how it came to be took over. She became an INFN researcher in Naples and has been researching cosmic rays for over 25 years, participating in the Auger experiments in the Argentine Pampas and at the Cherenkov Telescope Array in the Canary Islands.
Supernovas, p. 34

LIVIA CONTI

Researcher at the INFN in Padua since 2008, Livia Conti, since her high school years, has fostered an interest in the fundamental questions about humankind and our role in the Universe. She conducts experimental research in the field of gravitational wave detectors. Since 2014 she has been part of the Virgo collaboration that detects gravitational waves.
Spacetime and Gravitational Waves, pp. 8-9

FRANCESCO D'ERAMO

Professor of Physics at the University of Padua and member of the INFN, as a child Francesco D'Eramo wanted to be a footballer. Instead of the World Cup, however, he participated in the Physics Olympiad, where a new passion was born in him. After ten years in the United States he is happy to be back at work in Italy.
The Universe, pp. 2-3; The Big Bang, pp. 4-5; The Structure of the Universe, pp. 6-7; Galaxies, pp. 10-11

FRANCESCO 'FRANZ' LONGO

Professor of Physics at the University of Trieste and member of the INFN in gamma ray experiments, Francesco Longo felt a passion for the sky that slowly bourgeoned, thanks to 'stargazing' with the scouts and reading an illustrated history book on how ancient peoples imagined the sky they observed.
Neutron Stars, p. 35

ELISA PRANDINI

Researcher at the University of Padua and member of the INFN, Elisa Prandini works mainly with black holes and gamma rays. As a child she was undecided between being an archaeologist or a speleologist, but enchanted by a walk in the moonlight, she decided to become a physics researcher to study the Universe.
Extreme Universe, pp. 32-33

© 2021 Sassi Editore Srl
Viale Roma 122/b
36015 Schio (VI) - Italy

INFN collaboration: Sabine Hemmer and Anna Dalla Vecchia
Text adaptation: Irena Trevisan
Illustrations: Mattia Cerato
Layout: Alberto Borgo
Translation: SallyAnn DelVino

POSTER
50x70cm (19.7"x27.6")